How to use communication & NLP

Manipulating and leading the human mind trough different NLP techniques

C&I Consultants
Written by Babak Parvizi
Copyright© 2015
The Hague
The Netherlands

How to use communication & NLP, Manipulating and leading the human mind trough different NLP techniques provides the reader a basic understanding and advanced knowledge about different aspects of communication and how to use it for his favor. Of course it is a tool to use in good purposes. How many times does it happen that sales people want to increase their sales, while the key to their success lies in the way they communicate with the buyer. The same is applicable for managers and leaders who do not only want to give orders, but to change the drive of their employees. It is also a useful tool at home between a husband and a wife and with colleagues and friends. When you know what the drive is of the opposite person and the communication preferences then you will be able to build rapport, convince and set new goals as you like. There are three types of communication styles which is: visual, auditory and kinesthetic. And in this book we will further explain on how hypnotherapy and NLP (neuro linguistic programming) is used in presentations. NLP is a widely known technique about communication and persuasiveness.

I hope you enjoy reading this book and make it a useful tool to gain better results in the future.

Table of content

Introduction

Dear reader, during several years of study at the university, working many years in sales and specializing in communication as a tool for reaping more success I saw that many people struggle with communication. It could be that a husband and wife argue while with a better way of communicating with each other the problem could be solved. Sales people who earn a living and generate revenue as they are the face of the company need to master the skills of communication which breaks down to 3 parts: perceiving, analyzing and practicing the techniques explained. During my job in sales I was asked to coach people get better results. The area manager saw the results between colleagues and me, as I got the highest scores selling and earning different goods and services. The only difference between me and my colleagues was my mindset and the way I did things. Leaders and presentators often give speeches in front of people, they have to motivate a team. Different management styles have been analyzed but there are great results being achieved with leaders using communication in their favor. It is a art and when you master this art, you will become like a story teller where people enjoy listening to. Not forgetting the fact that the story has to include information, talking without actually saying something useful is like a man spitting thin air.

In the 21st century things have become more complex in life, and people talk about lifelong learning to achieve better results in their lives.
Are you that person? Than I wish you good luck and much pleasure in the understanding of the complex world called communication.

Because as Napoleon Hill said:

"The starting point of all achievement is DESIRE. Keep this constantly in mind. Weak desire brings weak results, just as a small fire makes a small amount of heat."

and

"Words are singularly the most powerful force available to humanity. We can choose to use this force constructively with words of encouragement, or destructively using words of despair. Words have energy and power with the ability to help, to heal, to hinder, to hurt, to harm, to humiliate and to humble. -Yehuda Berg "

and

"Take advantage of every opportunity to practice your communication skills so that when important occasions arise, you will have the gift, the style, the sharpness, the clarity, and the emotions to affect other people.- Jim Rohn"

and

"Before success comes in any man's life, he is sure to meet with much temporary defeat, and, perhaps, some failure. When defeat overtakes a man, the easiest and most logical thing to do is to quit. That is exactly what the majority of men do. More than five hundred of the most successful men this country has ever known told the author their greatest success came just one step beyond the point at which defeat had overtaken them." - Napoleon Hill

About the author

A long time ago a life of a young man started in the middle east. He was born in a Persian state, grown in a middle class family. This family flee away because of economical disturbance in the 90's to a small European country. The young man grew and got older, as he got older he got interested in finance and entrepreneurship. As he got to the point of going to the university, he made the decision to study international economics and business. During his study he worked in sales and was active in the local political community, he was good at it and wanted to bring the sales activities to a higher level. He graduated from the university, started working in a bank for a short time. He got a good job, saved and later on started his own firm in accounting and consulting and had multiple sources of income. In all those years in his life, he understood that communication skills are one of the most important if not the most important factor in life. Weather it is in personal relationships, in politics, sales, teaching, entrepreneurship and many others. In the past decades the way of communication has increased to a more sophisticated level to a extend that if you are not good at it. It will be seen as not socially accepted or you will get labeled as a introvert or not communicative person. Even engineers and software programmers have to create a decent level of social capabilities if they want to attract investment from venture capitalists for example.

Using communication in sales, relationships and team management

In this chapter we are going to focus on why and in which situations communication is important. And when persisting in something to master that skills, you will reap success and enjoy the fruits of your labor. There is a old saying about success which is:

"I'm convinced that about half of what separates the successful entrepreneurs from the non-successful ones is pure perseverance." - Steve Jobs

All people have their ups and downs in life, but the only thing that differs people is pure persistence. It is logical that some people are favored more than others, think about your background, family values, family status, money, the teachings of your parents and your environment. These will influence your personality and your future life. But no matter how strange or difficult your situation is. You can always change your skills and thus the outcome of your life in every aspect as you may wish.

"Communication is a skill that you can learn. It's like riding a bicycle or typing. If you're willing to work at it, you can rapidly improve the quality of every part of your life. – Brian Tracy"

Using communication skills in sales.

When you work as a sales person, more than 80 percent of what you say and do is about communication. Which means that only 20 percent of what you say is about the actual product or service. For example, you can say a few important things about the product but if your way of welcoming the customer and explaining it is not friendly. The customer will most likely get the product from somewhere else. Your non verbal signs have to be open, to build a certain trust in the opposite person. Customers now a day have the opportunity to not only purchase a product in a store but also online. Why should he/she buy something more expensive than somewhere else where it is cheaper. It is all about customer experience. In order to understand this we fist unfortunately have to understand the other person. The customer it self works very hard, maybe that person works in a hectic and boring office where he does not get any attention. After a few moths of saving and looking forward to purchasing a car or a tablet for example he comes to your store. There are two options:

1. You do not welcome the customer with a friendly open attitude. The customer does not get a welcome feeling and gets the feeling that he/she does not get appreciated. Hence he will go to a other shop where he can get a better service.

- You welcome the customer in a friendly manner, let him look around for a few seconds and ask what his questions are and where you can give advice on. While the customer explains that he is looking for a car, you ask him about the reason and for what purpose he is going to use it. While he explains that he is going to use his car for his work. You can ask in a decent manner that it is a good reason and you have different products which you are going to show him. In the meanwhile you aks about his job. He could be a entrepreneur. This is a win win situation. As a communicative person you can get info on the way others live. For instance I had customers who opened my eyes about new experiences. About travels which they made, their hobbies like flying a airplane, diving and many more. They showed me their pictures. This will have a positive impact in your life because you not only have the information on the things which you do in life. But it will open your eyes on many opportunities. Customers also told me about their entrepreneurial life and seeking for investors and selling their graphical service. A new world for a person which studied accounting, he will not know that there are many graphical designers having much free time and earning a decent amount of money and having a dynamic job.

The other win situation is for the customer. Why does he like it. We humans are social animals and we used to live in herds. Now in the 21st century as the society gets more complex and individualistic we do not need to life in a herd to survive. We do not life in a jingle with lions around us. Trough social security and a decent education you will have the ability to survive. Unfortunate for the alpha males which have to learn new skills like me and you in stead of hunting. Going back to the customer, he will have the chance to talk about his experiences, and believe me. More than 80percent of my customers enjoyed talking about the things which they did. Psychologically he will also get the feeling that he is accepted which means that his self esteem will increase. This is also in your case. Apple employees are very good at this. When you go to the apple store it is not only a person doing something for you, answering your questions. But also a personal experience as many people unconsciously have the need for this. I find Apple products too expensive and you pay for the design, most of their customers except the graphical designers and programmers do not use the functions which Apple provides. But look at the success and the profit which Apple has created in the past few years.

Using communication in team management.
Many times I have found my self in a position that I had to lead or manage others. In project groups at the university, in my job and in my side activities where I was the co-founder of a junior political group. There are 2 types of managers.
1 The Manager
2 The Leader

The manager manages his team by dividing tasks and giving orders. This is not motivating as many employees do not see a engaging team. i.e. they do not get the full experience that they are being appreciated and making a difference in their daily tasks. Of course there has to be a certain managing experience. I will elaborate on this topic. In the university we had project groups, as you may know many students are demotivated and lazy. Specially when it is a international environment you have to deal with people with different backgrounds. Backgrounds which include a siesta given in Spain or Diffuse relationships and high context communicating in Africa. Some people talk and do little, some people do not talk and do nothing, some people do not talk but to their task if it has to be done. The project groups in the fist year of college was a big point of frustration because people where not eager to do things. When I was chosen as a group leader I made the point that:
- we have to to the tasks efficient
- divide the task
- show results every 2 weeks
- make punishment if results or not there

This resulted in a very productive group work. The reason for this was that we first came together and discussed many things but did not make any progress. It looked like family chit chats. We did not divide the tasks, and different people have different skills which means if you point the task to the person with that skill, that person will enjoy the task and fulfill it in a good manner. Every 2 weeks show results in a short group meeting. Some people always delay things to the last moment, this will lead to a low quality result. You can give feedback on their results so that they can improve. And if they did not do the task, they will not enjoy the same grade as the others which do their task of their project. First a yellow card is given and the second time they are kicked out. This is a hard way but very productive for demotivated students. When he sees that the rest of the group gets a grade and she has to do a resit, this will not happen a second time.

This is called managing, but this could be also demotivating. I always pleat for a combination of managing, engaging and leading.

In my job there where employees much more experienced than me and having other competencies and interests than me. I am a good sales person, the other one was introvert and accurate and the other person very hectic. The hectic person became the so called middle manager and the introverted person became responsible for the back office. The positive thing was that every time I asked them to do certain tasks, I asked friendly: Lets do this as a team, can you do this, and you this and when I finish I will help you. This gave them the feeling that we are working as a team towards a goal. When the day was over I thanked them for their persistence and hard work. They asked me why I thank them for what they have to do and I explained that it was because they did their best as a team. This resulted in a higher team motivation and that they fulfilled their tasks every time in a better and faster way. And after we were finished we had time to talk about personal things like extra education, weekend activities and hobbies. I also did a internship in a dank where there was no group feeling at all. After a year consultants came to reduce costs and analyze which departments should increase productivity. They gave a report with information about the company culture, they said that it was a choking culture. Individualistic, demotivating and surviving culture.

Using communication in personal relationships.
Lets say that you are tired of your wife cooking bad food, or the same food every week. You can moan about it and increase your voice while saying: I do not want to eat this food, what is this! Or you can sit down and ask her to focus on the point you want to discuss with her. You explain the benefits of different food variety and the enjoyment of tasty food. You also point out the fact that it is very important for her health for the long run, and that you as a team want to enjoy even the smallest things in life. Some things are out of your hands, for example being a CEO is not something you can get if you want. But enjoying a tasteful food is. You go to the supermarket with her and choose different new food products that you as a team can explore. This is a very energy intensive process but it will result in a increased point of satisfaction and results. She will be more willing to change things. Of course you will have women who say in the end: cook your food your self. But in that case you choose the wrong spouse.

To make a conclusion, there is no such thing a failure. You will have a temporary defeat, and maybe multiple ones till you reach your goal. Your goal can be to becoming a entrepreneur, creating a big self running company, generate more sales or increase the quality of personal relationships.

Education

When some of us had no education and some of us had a good education and a high university degree. I don't find anything educative in a diploma. Of course I went to the university and I learned different things. Thing which I could not learn If I did not went there. But that is because of the people I met. If I got the books and learned by my self I would get the same amount of information, maybe even better. That is exactly what I did, my education did not start and end in the university. I started to read educative books when I was 16 and never finished. While many people study medicine, to become a doctor or a accountant. The only thing which they can do I calculating or making medicine. They lack on other aspects of life. I have different skills which also includes IT skills. I can build a computer from different parts and install a software on it like mac or windows. These people are mostly programmed to do one thing, and they lack different skills, even in their personal lives. I will give you a example. My mother told me for finding a good wife: son that lady will be a good wife, she goes to the university. What type of rationalizing is that. At that time I still lacked some knowledge because it was before my gradation. But that same girl was not religious which means that she will lack some norms and values what holds the family ties together. She lived by her self on a young age, and worse than that she did not do that for the right purposes. And to make it even more dirty, she borrowed every month to live on her own while she was studying. I know that many people do that. But as it is written in the book: a guide to think clearly. And I acknowledge that point which is that if 50.000 people do something, that same thing is still bad. No matter how many people do that. So on other things about that girl is that she lacked cooking and household things. I saw her after she started to live by her self and she looked worse by the day. Well what type of mother will that be to my children and what profit will I have from having her as a wife! In stead such person can get educated on different life aspects, eating and living healthy. Adapting good religious values for her future, she will be the first one to make a profit out of it. She could also read books on self improvement like you are doing now. At a young age around 16 and 17 I learned about saving and even putting my savings in a other country because the interest rates were higher there. Interest is no go in Islam and there is a good reason for it, the rich get richer and the poor poorer, so I stopped later on. And I learned about investing in the stock market, how to analyze the stocks on fundamental and technical analysis and later on derivative products. Then during my study I specialized in sales, communication, hypnotherapy and NLP. I practiced this during my presentations and student job and lo. The results were great, my manager was happy with my sales, at the university classmates asked me to pitch the presentation towards the teachers and so on. The reason that I am giving real life examples is to show you nothing comes for free, you have to become more conscious and greedy on knowledge to create a better life. During my study I worked as a sales person and I saw that the sales have to increase but I did not know how. So I started again and read different books about communication, nlp, marketing, sales. Guess what, at that company I became famous for being a top sales person. And some years later I gained approximate 30% extra salary every moths because of high bonuses, and no matter what I did. My employer liked me because I was the number 1 sales person in insurances in the whole area.

So educate your self, on you personal circumstances and your basic life which comes naturally. And educate your self about marketing, advertising sales. How different entrepreneurs started. It sounds tiring because you have to do all this research and reading. But it comes with the time, time is going no where, you get older by the day and you might spend your time in a wise manner. Weather it is entertainment, relaxation, education or work. Spend your time effective, efficient and wisely. You will have a long life so you can start now and over a few yours you will look back on how much knowledge you have gained by that time when every body else did nothing. I also want to let you know that you should not become too greedy and materialistic, because then you will lose your self. And forget your life purpose, money and work are just tools to have a better fulfilling life that you may spend more on charity, spend time with your family and enjoy life in a good way.

As a conclusion, life has different aspects. You can look at a thing in 2 ways or you can look in 3d and see what the other aspects are. So you may want to bring more consciousness on your friends and relationships, your marriage, your finances, healthy eating habits and going to the gym. Which somebody told me all those things, it would spear me a lot of effort finding things out by my self.

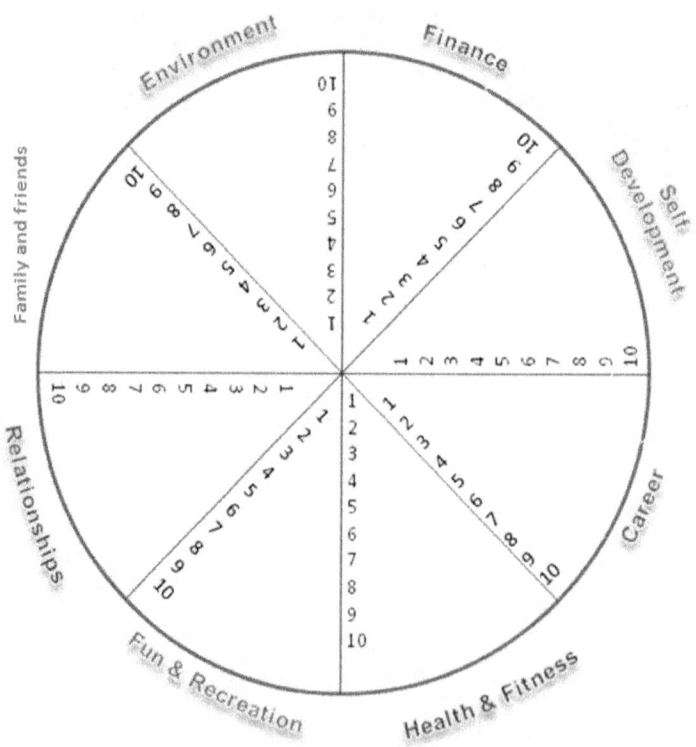

NLP

This part will be the most exotic part of this book. You will learn what NLP is and how to practice it. The point is not to use this in your daily conversations in family relationships. But it is good to be aware of it. It is mostly used in marketing/advertising and short presentations.

NLP stands for:
N= Neuro which means under the surface
L= Linguistic which means trough verbal communication
P= Programming which means how to simply program

In shot it means how to program or convince the other person unconsciously trough verbal expressions. But non verbal communication techniques is also used which we will explain shortly after these chapters.

While we communicate in our every day life we are unaware of how big the impact is of our words used. For example, a person who uses positive motivational words and thinks in a positive strategic way is more likely to search for things in life to increase productiveness, happiness or success in any given way. It is not only positive words, but when you have a positive attitude and you act like it, it will unconsciously stimulate your self and others around you to a higher goal.

You can use NLP in selling, negotiating, appraising, resolving conflict, presentations, coaching, serving customers, team work and motivating others.

When I was selling electronic products I noticed that some people want to watch the product and some people talk very fast. When for example giving a address to a person I always want to paint a map while others prefer to explain in simple words. This is called communication styles which is explained in NLP. Men mostly tend to be visualized, you can see that when we look at a nice looking lady. Our neck almost break when looking back at her while she passes by. But women do not get so much excited when looking at men, at least I do not think so. Women prefer romantic soft words. Men tend to look at women when sharing the bed so to say. And women want to hear nice words which is not duable for men because we focus on one thing. Just an extra point on focus, focusing means that you are mindful concentrating on one aspect. It is not always appreciated in the 21st century but it should be. Focusing leads to a higher productivity and less mistakes. When I went to my hairdresser to get a haircut. He was talking to the phone, cutting my hair and commanding his employees at the same time. Guess what, when I came home my hair did not look as a straight cut surface but instead it had loopholes and ups and downs like I just woke up.

To focus on NLP again, advertisers try to manipulate us or rhetorically said convince us trough our emotions and visual slides that this is the right product. For example, why do you not see a grandpa and a grandma drinking a martini and explaining the cold facts about this drink. Instead it shows a body builder men making the drink while the music bounces and the nice looking woman in the red dress getting attracted to one and another. This is simply called manipulation. The thing men desire is a nice looking woman, and the wife likes the men. When a group of ladies looks at this advertising before going out. This advertisement puts something called a "anchor" in the unconscious part of their brain that the thing which they are looking for. Which is romance, excitement and sex. Is just around the corner when drinking martini tonight in the club. Very unfortunate for the nice old couple we mentioned before drinking martini at their place surrounded by books and other old valuable things.

In the past I had a customer and he explained what his job was. Simply the lightning of parties, clubs and disco's. What he explained was that the color of the light can change the mood, while showing green or soft blue colors at a party the people were relaxed and more enjoyable. When changing the light to a red color mixing it with hard rock music it created a fundamental base for proactive people jumping and eventually some fights.

As a conclusion it is also important that people have communication styles, but these can change when having different moods. A person can be kinesthetic and later on be more focused on visual aspects.

Auditory

As we mentioned above, some people are auditory/ auditive. Which means they prefer sounds above visual or emotional signals. Auditive people mostly use the word: listen, explain and talk in their words. For example. My wife said:" Mister y, come over here and listen to what I have to say. When talking to your parents, they sounded stressful."

Auditory people mostly have fluctuating speed in their conversations. When your spouse is a auditory person and you want to discuss important things it would be wiser if you say to her: "I want to **discuss** a few things with you, and I would like you to sit down and **listen carefully** to what I have to **say**."

When using this sentence, the focus of this sentence is sound, listening and talking. It is important to use these words because you will use the same communication pattern as hers and it will lead to a better conversation.

Or lets say that you sale cars, you can use these sentences. "As you **said** what you want in your next car, which should have these important items like ...., I would like to show you this .... Peugeot because of the things you want in that car. This car is very **quit** when driving on the highway, it gives a certain **relaxation**, this is due to the new tire and motor techniques which makes the car a enjoyable car when driving even long trips.

When giving a speech or a presentation you can say:
As you sit in your **comfortable** chair, **listening** to the **sound** of my **voice**, I would like you to **focus** on the positive things which I have to **say** about ....

When you ask them about something in the past, auditory people have to think about it to recall that evening. When thinking, their eyes switch from the left to the right side or vice versa. They do not look up or down.

When communicating, 7% of the influence you can give is trough words. This is a small fraction considering that 38% is triggered by the tone of voice and 55% by facial expressions/posture or gestures.

Imagined or constructed sounds

Rembered sounds

Words used:
Tell me
I hear that
sounds like
so you say
tone
discuss

The breathing:
The breathing takes place trough the diaphragm

The tempo of speech:
Fluctuating

Visual

Visual people tend to look at things, their focus is on what they see or what they imagine. I am a visualized person, a few days ago I had a conversation about playing tennis. The other person asked me where I played tennis, I did not know the street name, but I mentioned that I can draw a map. Even when meeting new people I can not remember their names, only after a few weeks practicing and putting much effort in it I will remember it. That is why I draw the room and the seats where me and my new colleagues sit. On the seats I wrote down the names of my new colleagues, this was much easier for me and within a short period of time I remembered the names. Not mentioning the fact that when a beautiful lady passes by, we men do not thing about her voice, that is of no importance. We turn our necks and risk a hernia to have a better look on what just passed by. It is also known that because of many years of evolution, because we men were hunters. We had to look far in the fields to find a animal and hunt him. We have a smaller wide of view and we tend to look far away. Or at least not see what is close to our selves. Small things get unnoticed. For example: when your wife or girlfriend uses make up or just had a haircut, it will mostly not seen by men. My mother had a habit to change the place where the couch was and the television once in a while. When I came home from school or work I did not saw it. I comfortably sat down and ate my meal and my mother would ask me if I do not see anything. These are some small things which happen in every day life.

Going back to visual people, we mentioned that 55% of communication and impression which you leave behind comes trough facial expressions and gestures. When having a conversation it is very important to but a friendly face and open your hands to show your openness and leave a good impression. This does not count when you want to make a statement when you are furious. When you are selling or giving presentations, analyze what your customers communication preferences are, does he uses the word "see" or does he looks up when you ask him something or when he thinks about something. If he has a preference on visualized communication style you could use the sentences below.

When you sell things or give a presentation to visualized people you could use these sentences:
As you can **see** this sheet it **appears** that there are a few **graphs** about the current economic situation. And I would like you to **visualize** what you like to **see** in the upcoming years. My **vision** is that economic growth comes from hard work, higher production and more **focus** on sustainable improvements.

As you can **see** these jeans, it has a dark colored **painting** which is very **deeply** in the cotton. This is very good when you want to wash your pants and keep the new intense **color.** It **appears** as a semi casual pants, you can imagine wearing these pants on a Friday afternoon during work lunch, or when you go to a nice **looking** restaurant with your spouse.

Visual people tend to say the sentences like this:
What can you see.
Did you saw..
How does that appear to you?
Just imagine that...
How do we have to look and dress on that party?

Word that visual people use are like:
See
focus
big picture
viewpoint
perspective
vision
perceive
color
enlighten
look out
appear to

Voice:
Fast

Eyes

Visual constructed images

Visual remembered images

Kinesthetic

Kinesthetic people tend to communicate trough feelings. They emphasize the feelings which come to surface. For example, my fiancée said that she is not feeling happy, and that she feels there is something wrong. Because I spoke in a certain way. She wanted me to be more romantic and say things in a friendlier way. There is a personality test called MBTI. With this test you can see if you have feeler personality or a thinker. A thinker tries to analyze things, evaluate and practice. But feelers sympathize with other people, look on things which make them feel happy or sad. Social workers have a high EI or also called EQ. EI stands for emotional intelligence. They understand how others feel and their empathy is very strong.

When you sell products or services to people you can say these sentences, it is important that you say the fat cursed words in a slow motion, but not so slow that the person recognizes that you do this intentionally:

As you can **feel** how **enjoyable** it would be, you and your spouse sitting **comfortably** on a chair on the beach. It will be very **warm** around 30 **degrees** and while you drink your **cold ice** tea you will have a very **nice** view on the white beaches in Turkey.

As you **feel** these **heavy** pants, it is made from one of the **best** cotton qualities. It is waved in a **thick** way, you can **feel** how **heavy** these **whey**. In the winter, it will still give a **warm feeling** when wearing these pants.

Sentences like:
Being pleased
Do you have a bad day?
What are your ambitions?
Do you like these things?

Words:
Feel
impact
support
touch
warm
solid
hard
flow
heated
pressure
rough

Breath:
Deep

Voice:
Slow

 kinaesthetic (feelings and sensations)

Building rapport trough pacing and leading

What is building rapport? When people communicate or just meet each other it often happens that a person does not like or trust the other person. Did you have this feeling or intuition before? There are two ways to see if the other person is a good trust able person or not. One way is to analyze the personality, norms and values. For example if you know somebody who is not trustworthy, looking at your wife, wanting to steel something from your house or being jealous. It takes a lot of effort and knowledge to analyze these behaviors and come to a conclusion. This way of analyzing is very good for new things like choosing the right education or employer to work for. But in case of other humans we have created a faster way to analyze this. Its called intuition. Intuition is not always right, but my experience is that in the past four years it has always been right in my case. Which means you should not ignore it. This intuition is deeply rooted in the back of your brain. It was a survival mechanism many years ago. If someone in the group was not trustworthy in the stone age, when we lived in herds. It could get you killed for example during haunting.

Building rapport means that you and the other person trust each other and even like each other maybe. Have you seen a couple sitting at a bar. They lean the same way behind or to the front. Their legs are mostly the same way crossed or open. Their body language is copied on both sides. When we trust another person and even like the other personality we tend to use the same body and non verbal suggestions as him/her.

Building rapport should come naturally, if you copy every move the other person makes it would not make a good impression. Believe me. But if you see that the other person is trustworthy and you want to build rapport. You can smoothly copy the most important body language like the way they sit. After a few minutes having a nice conversation and building rapport you can lead the other person. This means that the other person unconsciously sees you also as a trustworthy person and automatically follows you body language.

Anchors for persuasiveness

Anchors are very important if you want to persuasive the other person. For example if you want to persuasive the teachers or investors to invest in your company or want to convince the other person. It works in both presentations and sitting conversations.

So what are anchors. A anchor is a move, place, product or word that you associate with something. For example: you want to convince the investor to invest in your company. When you walk to the right side of the room you say all the negative things in the economy and which can happen. When you walk to the left side of the room you say all the positive things in the economy. Not forgetting to mention positive emotions and a the feeling which the investor could get when earning a high profit and laying on the beach in the Bahama's. Then you walk to the middle of the room and say that the investor is looking for a good product to invest in with a high return. Right? After that you walk again to the left part of the room and present your product and explain this is the solution to the needs of the society!

Did you get the point? Unconsciously the right side of the room was associated with negative aspects. The left side was associated with positive future aspects and positive feelings. After that you walked to the middle of the room to neutralize and question the situation. Then you walked again to the left side of the room to show the solution which was your product. Your product will be associated with all the positive aspects which the investors would like to see and achieve. You can also use your right hand and left hand to show what is good and what is not, or use other anchors.

I also used these anchors to help a girl accept and minimize a negative thing which happened in her past. So it could be very useful. There was a round orange paper on the left side of her. And a light blue colored paper in a square shape on the right side. She stood in the middle and I asked her to get in a deep relaxation, while imagining this situation feeling a deep certain sensation. Then walk to the left side and stand on the orange round paper. Imagine that moment. Hear the sounds. How was the feeling. If you want to get rid of it, you just see a picture of that moment, hold the picture in your mind and see it go further from you. As the picture goes further away you will see just a point. All the negative have become more transparent and relax. Now you move to the middle and relax, neutralize the emotions and see things as they are now. Just nothing but relax. After that go to the right side and stand on the blue square. This is a solid positive color. Imagine how you want things to be, see the situation in a big colored picture. Get the feeling how the positive emotion will become. What sounds will you hear or say. Then walk again to the middle and imagine that the same big picture will become more solid. The positive things which you imagine will become more in the present.

This is a way to minimize unconsciously a negative thing in your brain and stimulate a positive thing for the future. It will be like a seed planted in the brain of the other person. If this will be practiced a few times and the person is a proactive hard working person. There will be positive results created from this.

Non verbal communication

As we mentioned earlier, around 80percent of our perceiving in human interactions come from non verbal communication. What does this mean? The words you use and the content which you are explaining is important. But the thing which influences the other person the most is the way you look, body language and impression which you make.

I remember that I was around 17 years when I saw this beautiful young woman walking in a store. We looked at each other and that was it. The friend which was talking to me got ignored and he punched me while saying that he still was talking and I had to focus, but of course I didn't heard anything any more. So I walked up to the lady and said in a Dutch language that I found her one of the best looking woman I have ever seen. She replied me with:Entschuldigung! She was German and didn't understand anything which I said. But it went very well and we dated a couple of months. The point which I want to make is that I was not explaining Shakespeare. The first thing which matters is the open non verbal signs you give.

Arms: A open arm and showing your hands is a open sign. It shows non consciously that you are not hiding something. Crossed arms however do not stimulate any conversation and is known as a haughty sign.

Legs: When legs are crossed it is also perceived as a haughty personality. That you are better than the other person. When our feet point to the person we are talking to, it shows that we are interested, and when our feet are pointed the other way it shows we do not have any intention of communicating with that person.

Sometimes you have the ability to choose what you are going to do. If you see someone and you do not like or trust that person. You can just look the other way and show that you are not interested in any communication. But if you want to build relationships and show a open posture. You can easily open your arms, smile and point your legs in the direction of the other person.

This may look well-known, but it is good to be aware of it.

Hypnotherapy in presentations
Now we know how the differences are in human interaction like auditive, visual and kinesthetic. And the fact that we have to build rapport trough non verbal communication and using anchors to persuasive someone, we should know how to practice this in a presentation.

Lets say that you have a corporate job, giving a sales pitch to a other company or to some investors. How are you going to do that besides the practical matters like a good power point sheet and a informative content.

The people have to feel comfortable, trust you and get persuade that your solution is the right solution they are looking for. How are you going to do that? I will write a example of a presentation and show which word have the most effect on:
-The relaxation of that person
-Building trust
-communicate on the same way
-using anchors

You stand in the middle of the room. Welcome everyone, **thank** you for being here spending your time for this **important** topic. As you **will sit in your comfortable** chair, **listening** to the **sound** of **my voice**. I would like you to **relax** and **look** to the presentation which I am going to **show** you while you **hear** the **detailed explanations** which I am going to **present**. We are going to **explain** the next topics.......

You walk to the left side of the room. As we **heard** what impact the recent **crisis** had on peoples lives. We **saw** that people had **problems** with ..... Considering the **fact** that our company **focuses** on other products and **needs** of people and companies we **saw** this **great opportunity seeing** the big **picture**.

You walk to the right side of the room.
After we **focused** on this **solid** product..... We **discussed** it
with colleagues and customers. Their **feedback** and
enthusiasm was of **great importance** to us. An we became
more **aware** of this **great opportunity** having a **solid** solution
and the **feeling** that people get **satisfied**.

You walk to the middle or left and explain again the **needs** of
the people and why the **problem** was bad.

Walk again to the right and say:
And gentlemen, while you also become **aware** of these
sensations you **see** the **positive impact** which we all can have.
This.... product/service which we offer is a **great solution**.
Explain the details and say that you can prove this fact
because you did research. Hence, we found this solution to
create a **win win** situation. And as the future will bring us a
steady conversion of earnings, straight in to cash. We would
like to you to work with us on this part and **create** a **great
impact** for that is what the future **holds** for us.

Thank you word

Remember that life is like a journey. You should not see it as a task. Enjoy that journey, because you will learn new things and practice that knowledge. When you use your competencies and feel in your element, that is the moment when you are the most productive and successful. Because you do what you like and that you are good at it in a playful way. As our society get more complicated, our technology, electronic products, relationships and even the way we communicate evolve and become more complex. We have to learn new things to become more productive and stay updated.

I hope this book provided you with all the necessary basic information about the way we communicate and how to practice it in your personal and corporate lives. You could always read more in depth about different things which I mentioned in this book. A wise man once said that a person with low self esteem tries and falls and never tries again. A person with a high self esteem is so persistent that he will try till he finally does not get defeated and wins! I wish you good luck, enjoyment and much success in the future.

www.ingramcontent.com/pod-product-compliance
Lightning Source LLC
Chambersburg PA
CBHW072314200526
45168CB00014B/1538